WOULD YOU RATHER BOOK FOR KIDS (VOLUME #1)

200 Challenging Choices, Silly Scenarios, and Side-Splitting Situations Your Family Will Love

Cooper the Pooper

2020 Books by Cooper

ALL RIGHTS RESERVED

No part of this book may be reproduced, stored in a retrieval system, or transmitted in any form or by any means, electronic, mechanical, photocopying, recording, or otherwise, without the prior written permission of the publisher.

TABLE OF CONTENTS

Table of Contents 3

Introduction 4

Chapter 1: The Human Body 10

Chapter 2: Animals 36

Chapter 3: Supernatural Powers 62

Chapter 4: Everything Else! 88

Thank You for Reading 114

INTRODUCTION

Have you ever wondered what would be worse? Having hands for feet or feet for hands?

Or what would be better? Having ears the size of ants, or having ants in your ears?

Well, if you like wondering about these crazy things and having a big old laugh in the process, I have got you covered. See, you currently hold in your hands one of my favorite pieces of work, being a book that contains more than 200 of my favorite "would you rather" questions. Trust me when I say these are not just any old questions. These are some of the most challenging, silly, and side-splitting questions on the planet. These questions will have you pulling your hair out in frustration. They will have you rolling around on the ground in laughter. And of course, they will have you so confused that you don't know which way is up.

Get ready to laugh at one of my finest pieces of work.

Now, I know what you are thinking – why would I read a book written by a dog?

And I get it.

See, not so long ago I was what you would consider a very normal dog. I spent most of my time chasing cats, digging holes, and having fun with the neighborhood kids. But then something bad happened.

Instead of playing with *me*, the local kids started spending all their time stuck inside playing video games.

I mean, how boring can you get?

So, I decided that something needed to change.

With this in mind, I started thinking of some great ways kids just like you can have *real* fun with your friends and family – and not just stare at a TV all day.

And this is when I decided to start writing books.
But not just any old books, mind you. Books that get you laughing. Books that get you thinking. Books that you can share with all your friends and family.

Books full to the brim with hilarious "would you rather" questions, for example.

I scoured the globe for the best questions in the world and put them into this book – this same book that you now hold in your hand.

And trust me when I say they are *good.*

What are you waiting for? Open the pages, and get laughing with your friends and family.

Also by Cooper The Pooper

- Would You Rather Game Book for Kids: 200 More Challenging Choices, Silly Scenarios, and Side-Splitting Situations Your Family Will Love (Vol 2)

- The Silly Kids Joke Book: 500+ Hilarious Jokes That Will Make You Laugh Out Loud!

- Would You Rather Game Book for Kids (Gross Edition): 200+ Totally Gross, Disgusting, Crazy and Hilarious Scenarios the Whole Family Will Love!

- Interesting Facts for Smart Kids: 1,000+ Fun Facts for Curious Kids and Their Families

- Difficult Riddles for Smart Kids : 400+ Difficult Riddles and Brain Teasers Your Family Will Love (Vol 1)

Get the Audiobook for Free!

If you enjoy listening to books while you're on the go, I have exciting news for you! You can download the audiobook version of "Would You Rather Game Book for Kids" absolutely free! Yes, completely free, simply by signing up for a 30-day trial on Audible at zero cost.

To begin, simply scan the QR code below.

Scan or visit -
www.booksbycooper.com/audible

Want Our Next Book for Free?

Simply enter your details on our sign-up page, and our next fun-filled book for kids will be yours to enjoy. It's easy, quick, and completely free. Don't miss out on this opportunity to add an exciting new book to your child's collection.

To begin, simply scan the QR code below.

Scan or visit - www.booksbycooper.com/next

SCAN ME

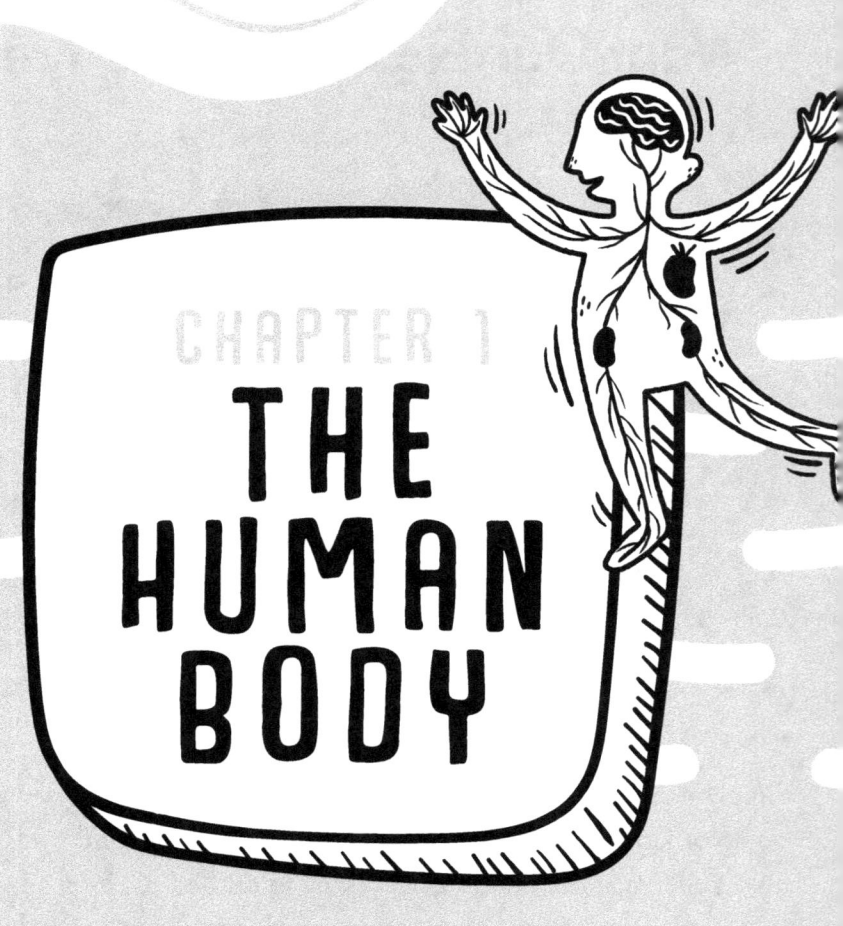

CHAPTER 1
THE HUMAN BODY

Let's start with the human body. You can't tell me you haven't ever imagined having an extra leg or no ears! Well, let's put it to the test then, with some classic "would you rather" choices.

The great thing about "would you rather" is that you always have to choose one of the answers for each question! That goes for all the questions: the ones where you want to pick both answers, and also the ones where you don't want to pick either answer!

The important thing is to weigh the good side and the bad side in your head before answering, so that you can make the smartest possible choice that you can explain if needed!

WOULD YOU RATHER...

01
Have four ears but no nose
- OR -
Four noses and no ears?

02
Have fingernails for eyelashes
- OR -
Eyelashes for fingernails?

WOULD YOU RATHER...

03

Poop from your mouth
- OR -
Eat through your bum?

04

Have an extra thumb on your left hand
- OR -
An extra finger on your right hand?

WOULD YOU RATHER...

05

Have spaghetti for arms
- OR -
Cucumbers for legs?

06

Have no ears
- OR -
One giant eye?

WOULD YOU RATHER...

07

Eat your boogers

- OR -

Swallow your fingernails?

08

Lick someone's ear

- OR -

Have someone lick your ear?

WOULD YOU RATHER...

09 You didn't fart but everyone thought you did

- OR -

Fart and blame your friend?

10 Have a tongue as long as our arm

- OR -

An arm as long as your tongue?

WOULD YOU RATHER...

11

Walk backward

- OR -

Walk on your hands?

12

No longer be able to speak

- OR -

No longer able to hear?

WOULD YOU RATHER...

13

Burp every time you blink
- OR -
Fart every time you sneeze?

14

Have one arm and three legs
- OR -
Three arms and one leg?

WOULD YOU RATHER...

15

Have no bottom

- OR -

No neck?

16

Have gills to breathe underwater

- OR -

Wings to fly in the sky?

WOULD YOU RATHER...

17

Everything tasted like broccoli

- OR -

You couldn't taste anything you ate?

18

Have no teeth but x-ray vision

- OR -

No lips but you can read people's minds?

WOULD YOU RATHER...

19

Never be able to say your name

- OR -

Have to say every fourth word backward?

20

Grow oranges out of your ears

- OR -

Apples out of your knees?

WOULD YOU RATHER...

21

Have the world's longest toenails

- OR -

The world's smallest fingers?

22

Only be able to say words that start with "B"

- OR -

Never be able to say three-letter words again?

WOULD YOU RATHER...

23

Your fingers were made of fish fingers

- OR -

Your toes were made of chips?

24

Your ears were made of cheese

- OR -

Your nose was made of chocolate?

WOULD YOU RATHER...

25
Not be able to say the letter "M" ever again

- OR -

Only ever be able to use words with an "A" in them?

26
Have another set of eyes in the back of your head

- OR -

Be able to run on all fours?

WOULD YOU RATHER...

27

Be completely covered in hair

- OR -

Be completely hairless all over?

28

Be joined at the hip to one of your parents

- OR -

Joined at the shoulder to your best friend?

WOULD YOU RATHER...

29 Have to whistle every time you say hi
- OR -
Never be able to say goodbye to anyone?

30 Have carrots for teeth
- OR -
Peppers for lips?

WOULD YOU RATHER...

31

Have ears where your eyes are

- OR -

Eyes where your ears are?

32

Have an extra arm but it is made out of jelly

- OR -

An extra leg that is made out of wood?

WOULD YOU RATHER...

33

Be ticklish every time someone touched you

- OR -

Be able to tickle anyone, even if they aren't ticklish?

34

Have ten toes on one foot and no toes on the other

- OR -

Eight toes on each foot?

WOULD YOU RATHER...

35

Be hilarious

- OR -

A smarty pants?

36

Be ten years older

- OR -

Three years younger?

WOULD YOU RATHER...

37

Taste sour milk

- OR -

Brush your teeth with lemon juice?

38

Have to walk like a crab

- OR -

Have to hop on one foot?

WOULD YOU RATHER...

39

Only be able to eat all your food as a blended drink

- OR -

Only eat food that is cold or not cooked?

40

Immediately become a grown-up

- OR -

Stay the same age for the next three years?

WOULD YOU RATHER...

41

Your eyes changed color depending on how warm it is

- OR -

Your hair changed color when you become happy or sad?

42

Continue to go to school until you're 80

- OR -

Turn 50 tomorrow?

WOULD YOU RATHER...

43

Be able to understand sign language

- OR -

Tell what people are saying by reading their lips?

44

Didn't have to eat another meal ever again

- OR -

Not have to sleep ever again?

WOULD YOU RATHER...

45

Forced to sneeze once every three minutes every day

- OR -

Sneeze non-stop for ten minutes every day?

46

Be stung once by a bee

- OR -

Stung five times by a mosquito?

WOULD YOU RATHER...

47

Be able to see a range of colors that others can't see

- OR -

Hear noises that other people can't hear?

48

Talk uncontrollably quickly

- OR -

Uncontrollably loudly?

WOULD YOU RATHER...

49
Be able to grow out your hair with your mind

- OR -

Grow your nails with your mind?

50
Never have to drink water again

- OR -

Never get tired, no matter how much you run around?

CHAPTER 2
ANIMALS

It's time to get a little wild! We all envy some of the fastest, loudest, and coolest animals out there, but which ones do you envy the most?

Have you ever wondered what in the world it would be like to have the head of a giraffe, or the body of a leopard?

Well, you don't need to wonder anymore! This chapter is packed with 50 different "would you rather" questions, all focused around the theme of animals.

Some of these questions will leave you wishing you could pick both, but sadly you are only allowed to choose one! That is the fun of playing "would you rather," after all.

And then there are some that you really won't want to answer, but you still have to! Let's get started.

WOULD YOU RATHER...

01
Have stripes like a zebra
- OR -
Spots like a leopard?

02
Tower as tall as a giraffe
- OR -
Be as strong as a bull?

WOULD YOU RATHER...

03

Be able to howl like a wolf

- OR -

Hoot like an owl?

04

Run like a cheetah

- OR -

Fly like an eagle?

WOULD YOU RATHER...

05

Live with elephants
- OR -
Rhinos?

06

Speak all human languages
- OR -
Be able to speak to animals?

WOULD YOU RATHER...

07

Have paws for hands
- OR -
Hooves for feet?

08

Be able to swing through trees like monkeys
- OR -
Jump like a kangaroo?

WOULD YOU RATHER...

09

Have a hyena as an evil nemesis

- OR -

A baboon as a best friend?

10

Have fur as soft as a cat

- OR -

Hair as spikey as a hedgehog?

WOULD YOU RATHER...

11

Be as lazy as a sloth
- OR -
As tubby as a hippo?

12

Be able to swim like a dolphin
- OR -
Fly like a woodpecker?

WOULD YOU RATHER...

13

Have a camel's hump
- OR -
An elephant's trunk?

14

Be hugged by a panda
- OR -
Hugged by a koala?

WOULD YOU RATHER...

15

Fight a bear
- OR -
Fight a tiger?

16

Have a pet cow
- OR -
A pet sheep?

WOULD YOU RATHER...

17

Live underground like a mole

- OR -

Live in a tree like a squirrel?

18

Be as big as a whale

- OR -

As little as a mouse?

WOULD YOU RATHER...

19

Have the trunk of an elephant

- OR -

The beak of a pelican?

20

Have to eat bacon every day

- OR -

Never eat bacon ever again?

WOULD YOU RATHER...

21

Smell like a skunk

- OR -

Smell like a dung beetle?

22

Leave a slime trail like a slug

- OR -

Only be able to move as fast as a snail?

WOULD YOU RATHER...

23

Fight a duck the size of a horse
- OR -
100 duck-sized horses?

24

Have to carry a baby kangaroo everywhere
- OR -
Be carried in a kangaroo's pouch?

WOULD YOU RATHER...

25

Be able to do tricks like a seal

- OR -

Run as fast as an antelope?

26

Be able to talk to cats

- OR -

Talk to dogs?

WOULD YOU RATHER...

27

A dog ruled the world

- OR -

A family of giant spiders lived next door?

28

Eat a live scorpion

- OR -

A live jellyfish?

WOULD YOU RATHER...

29

Have wings like a pigeon

- OR -

The stinger of a bee?

30

Be an ant that lives for 300 years

- OR -

A tiger that lives for 50 years?

WOULD YOU RATHER...

31

Turn into a fish every time it rains

- OR -

A bird every time it is windy?

32

Be a polar bear living in the desert

- OR -

A camel living in the arctic?

WOULD YOU RATHER...

33
Be an elephant trapped in a giraffe's body

- OR -

A giraffe trapped in an elephant's body?

34
Be able to swim with penguins

- OR -

Jump with kangaroos?

WOULD YOU RATHER...

35

Transform into a toad once a week

- OR -

Transform into a bird once a week?

36

Have wings but not be able to fly

- OR -

Have flippers but not be able to swim?

WOULD YOU RATHER...

37

Have a ride on a giant dog
- OR -
A tiny giraffe?

38

Have a pet cat
the size of an elephant
- OR -
A pet elephant
the size of a cat?

WOULD YOU RATHER...

39 Be able to know what animals are saying but not speak to them

- OR -

Animals understand what you are saying, but they can't talk to you?

40 Be cuddled by five kittens

- OR -

Five puppies?

WOULD YOU RATHER...

41

Be able to camouflage like a chameleon

- OR -

Be able to breathe underwater for a maximum of two hours?

42

Have a dragon as a pet

- OR -

A dinosaur?

WOULD YOU RATHER...

43

Ride a dolphin through the sea
- OR -
A lion through the Sahara Desert?

44

Have a pet robot dinosaur
- OR -
A real pet dinosaur?

WOULD YOU RATHER...

45

Be a zebra

- OR -

An antelope?

46

Your mom was an armadillo

- OR -

Your dad was a leopard?

WOULD YOU RATHER...

47

Eat a spider

- OR -

Let a wasp sting you?

48

Have a panda that's your best friend

- OR -

A zebra as a neighbor?

WOULD YOU RATHER...

49 Your sweat was the same as bee honey

- OR -

Always smell like a skunk, even after a shower?

50 Hug a grizzly bear

- OR -

Lick a frog?

CHAPTER 3
SUPERNATURAL POWERS

Imagine how much cooler life would be with superpowers! Well, now you have to choose which ones you think would make your life even more awesome!

We've pulled together 50 "would you rather" questions based around supernatural powers for you to answer. Some of them are good and you wish you had both options, and some of them are bad and you wish you had neither.

The main thing is, make sure you answer each and every single one of them!

WOULD YOU RATHER...

01
Have super hearing powers
- OR -
Be able to see through walls?

02
Be able to breathe underwater
- OR -
Be able to fly?

WOULD YOU RATHER...

03

Make it rain whenever you want

- OR -

Start a fire instantly?

04

Be a superhero

- OR -

A supervillain?

WOULD YOU RATHER...

05

Have super speed
- OR -
Super strength?

06

Be able to travel into the past
- OR -
See into the future?

WOULD YOU RATHER...

07

Be super-rich all the time
- OR -
Super-happy all the time?

08

Shoot arrows out of your eyes
- OR -
Cannonballs out of your knees?

WOULD YOU RATHER...

09

Jump as high as the moon

- OR -

Be able to fall from any height without hurting yourself?

10

Be able to make things disappear

- OR -

Move them without touching them?

WOULD YOU RATHER...

11

Read other people's thoughts
- OR -
Control what other people say?

12

Only see what you want to
- OR -
Remember everything you see?

WOULD YOU RATHER...

13 Be the most intelligent person in the world and nobody knows it

- OR -

Not be very clever, and everybody thinks you are really intelligent?

14 Shoot lasers out of your toes

- OR -

Run faster than the speed of light?

WOULD YOU RATHER...

15

Have super strength every time you eat carrots

- OR -

Fly every time you eat a grape?

16

See in the dark

- OR -

See underwater?

WOULD YOU RATHER...

17

Cut through glass with your fingernails

- OR -

Be able to write with your feet?

18

Shoot laser beams from your elbows

- OR -

Have rockets in your feet?

WOULD YOU RATHER...

19

Be able to control people's minds but not be able to walk

- OR -

Be able to walk and not have any superpowers?

20

Be able to travel back in time but be invisible

- OR -

Travel into the future and be the king or queen of the world?

WOULD YOU RATHER...

21
Be able to turn into a table
- OR -
Turn into a chair?

22
Be able to fly every time you ate a mushroom
- OR -
become super strong every time you eat sweetcorn?

WOULD YOU RATHER...

23

Be able to walk through walls but only when it is raining

- OR -

Breathe underwater but only at night?

24

Be able to teleport but not be allowed to speak to your family ever again

- OR -

Have super speed but leave a trail of mud everywhere you go?

WOULD YOU RATHER...

25

Be one of the Avengers

- OR -

Part of the Justice League?

26

Be the inventor of a sport for superheroes

- OR -

Be the inventor of a superhero holiday resort?

WOULD YOU RATHER...

27

Be the leader of an alien race on Mars

- OR -

Be the president of the United States?

28

Be able to see miles into the distance

- OR -

Have high definition vision at close range?

WOULD YOU RATHER...

29

Have super reading powers
- OR -
The power to speak really quickly?

30

Have an invisible submarine
- OR -
An invisible magic carpet?

WOULD YOU RATHER...

31

Be the best ninja in the whole world

- OR -

Know what everyone is thinking?

32

Be able to teleport but you have to wear a silly hat

- OR -

Be able to travel back in time but only if you are wearing a kilt?

WOULD YOU RATHER...

33
Have the power of super memory

- OR -

The power to perfectly imitate anyone's voice?

34
Be able to make origami that comes to life

- OR -

Be a real magician?

WOULD YOU RATHER...

35
Be able to grow as large as the tallest building

- OR -

Shrink to the size of an ant?

36
Be able to walk without making any sound

- OR -

Have a voice that is incredibly intimidating and scary?

WOULD YOU RATHER...

37

Be bulletproof

- OR -

Be able to jump from any height without getting hurt?

38

Be able to camouflage yourself anywhere at any time

- OR -

Be able to walk through walls?

WOULD YOU RATHER...

39

Be able to control all metal with your mind

- OR -

Be in control of the weather?

40

Be able to speak every language but not be able to write in any of them

- OR -

Be able to write in any language but be unable to speak?

WOULD YOU RATHER...

41

Be able to find anything that has ever been lost instantly

- OR -

Force people to tell the truth?

42

Be able to watch films in your mind by closing your eyes

- OR -

Read any book you want in your dreams?

WOULD YOU RATHER...

43

Be able to control what color everything in the world is

- OR -

Be the most popular person in the world?

44

Have the world's strongest legs

- OR -

The world's strongest arms?

WOULD YOU RATHER...

45
Have the power to never forget anything you read

- OR -

Never forget anything anyone says?

46
Have an unlimited supply of Lego

- OR -

Have any video game you want instantly?

WOULD YOU RATHER...

47

Have the power to choose if a coin lands on heads or tails

- OR -

Never lose a game of rock, paper, scissors?

48

Be the fastest typist in the world

- OR -

The best dancer?

WOULD YOU RATHER...

49

Learn from books by sleeping next to them in bed

- OR -

Be able to dream about whatever you want once a week?

50

Have a shrink ray that makes everything smaller

- OR -

A similar ray gun that makes everything bigger?

CHAPTER 4
EVERYTHING ELSE!

What about all the other fantastic "would you rather" questions? Well, fear not, we have pulled together all the very best ones that didn't fall into the previous categories. Sit back, have a good giggle, and ask your friends some of these fun questions.

This chapter has no theme, and only one single rule. You have to answer every single one, no skipping!

Some of these questions will be witty and entertaining for you to pick from; however, some of them will be gross and you won't want to choose either of them! But you have to pick, so try and pick the one that grosses you out the least!

WOULD YOU RATHER...

01

Have your own horse

- OR -

A swimming pool in the back garden?

02

Be the best painter in the world

- OR -

The best singer in the world?

WOULD YOU RATHER...

03

Do school work with your best friend

- OR -

On your own?

04

Be able to do backflips but fart each time

- OR -

Do front flips and burp each time?

WOULD YOU RATHER...

05

Shoot fireworks out of your armpits

- OR -

Be able to ride a unicycle with your hands?

06

It was boiling hot but raining

- OR -

Cold and snowy?

WOULD YOU RATHER...

07
Be a pirate
with your own ship

- OR -

A fighter pilot
with your own plane?

08
Design the best toy ever
but everyone thought it was
your friend who made it

- OR -

They made the best toy
and everyone thought it was
you that made it?

WOULD YOU RATHER...

09 Be really good at math
- OR -
Captain of the soccer team?

10 Write a book on how to eat mud
- OR -
Sing a song about the joy of peeing your pants?

WOULD YOU RATHER...

11

Have a house in the shape of a hexagon

- OR -

In the shape of a parallelogram?

12

Live in a forest

- OR -

Live underwater?

WOULD YOU RATHER...

13

Redecorate your room in whatever way you wanted

- OR -

Buy any toy you want?

14

Every wall in your house was the same color

- OR -

Every floor in your house was made of jelly?

WOULD YOU RATHER...

15

Spend a week living on the moon

- OR -

A week living on the sun?

16

Meet your favorite celebrity

- OR -

Have your own tv show?

WOULD YOU RATHER...

17 Have a room in your house that is full of bubbles

- OR -

A slide that goes from your roof into the backyard?

18 Dance in front of all of your classmates

- OR -

Sing in front of all of your teachers?

WOULD YOU RATHER...

19

Be really dumb but have lots of luck

- OR -

Be really smart and really unlucky?

20

Eat an entire lemon

- OR -

A raw potato?

WOULD YOU RATHER...

21
Have your own pet robot
- OR -
A jetpack with unlimited fuel?

22
Have no homework ever again
- OR -
Be given $5 by your school every time you do your homework?

WOULD YOU RATHER...

23

Eat spaghetti sauce but with no noodles

- OR -

Just the spaghetti noodles without any sauce?

24

Camp out next to a lake

- OR -

Go swimming with dolphins?

WOULD YOU RATHER...

25

All ice cream tasted like broccoli

- OR -

All cookies tasted like beef?

26

Your entire house was see-through

- OR -

You lived underground?

WOULD YOU RATHER...

27

Your money doubled every month

- OR -

You got $10 every morning just for waking up?

28

Be a firefighter

- OR -

A police officer?

WOULD YOU RATHER...

29

Open five small presents for a week

- OR -

One big present a week?

30

Be stuck in a room full of slugs

- OR -

Stuck in the bathtub with maggots?

WOULD YOU RATHER...

31

All the floors in your house be trampolines

- OR -

They all be aquariums with fish in them?

32

Your school got rid of tests

- OR -

Got rid of homework?

WOULD YOU RATHER...

33

Be stuck in quicksand

- OR -

Stuck in Nutella?

34

Have a freezer that produces ice cream magically

- OR -

A cupboard producing a chocolate bar magically?

WOULD YOU RATHER...

35

Find money in your drawer every day

- OR -

Eat pizza for breakfast every day?

36

Lick a dirty wall

- OR -

A clean toilet seat?

WOULD YOU RATHER...

37 Your team won every game, but you were the worst player

- OR -

Be the best player on a team that never wins?

38 Be fifteen years older

- OR -

Two years younger?

WOULD YOU RATHER...

39

Go on a holiday to Jupiter
- OR -
Go on a holiday to Mercury?

40

Have the loudest voice in the world
- OR -
The quietest voice in the world?

WOULD YOU RATHER...

41

Only be able to enter a room on your hands

- OR -

Always have to shout your own name when you leave a room?

42

Live in a penthouse in the middle of a busy city

- OR -

A large farm in the middle of nowhere?

WOULD YOU RATHER...

43

Meet your favorite cartoon character

- OR -

Your favorite Marvel superhero?

44

Drink an entire bottle of ketchup

- OR -

Drink an entire bottle of hot sauce?

WOULD YOU RATHER...

45
Never be able to listen to music again

- OR -

Never be able to watch a movie?

46
Not be able to watch television for twelve months

- OR -

Not be allowed to eat junk food for twelve months?

WOULD YOU RATHER...

47

Have to wash all the dishes after a meal

- OR -

Set the table before you eat each time?

48

Have a swimming pool of chocolate milk

- OR -

A bath of vanilla ice cream?

WOULD YOU RATHER...

49
Have salty Jell-O
- OR -
Sugary chips?

50
Go on a camping trip
- OR -
Stay in a fancy hotel?

THANK YOU FOR READING

Hi there!

Big thanks for reading our book. We're delighted to share the magic of "Would You Rather Game Book for Kids" with you.

Did you like the book? If you did, can you help us out? We'd be super happy if you could leave a review. This helps more kids and families find our books and enjoy them just like you did. To leave a review, simply scan the QR code below or head over to our website at booksbycooper.com/wyr-review.

Every review means a lot to us. Thank you for helping our small business grow!

Your friend,
Cooper

www.ingramcontent.com/pod-product-compliance
Lightning Source LLC
Chambersburg PA
CBHW071500070526
44578CB00001B/398